EXAMINING FOREST HABITATS

Zelda King

PowerKiDS
press™
New York

Published in 2009 by The Rosen Publishing Group, Inc.
29 East 21st Street, New York, NY 10010

First Edition

Editor: Joanne Randolph
Book Design: Kate Laczynski
Photo Researcher: Jessica Gerweck

Photo Credits: Cover, pp. 1, 11, 13, 15, 17 Shutterstock.com; p. 5 © www.istockphoto.com/Natalia Bratslavsky; pp. 7, 19 © Clip Art; p. 9 © www.istockphoto.com/Ina Peters; p. 21 © www.istockphoto.com.

Library of Congress Cataloging-in-Publication Data

King, Zelda.
  Examining forest habitats / Zelda King. — 1st ed.
      p. cm. — (Graphic organizers. Habitats)
  Includes index.
  ISBN 978-1-4358-2718-9 (library binding) — ISBN 978-1-4358-3122-3 (pbk.)
ISBN 978-1-4358-3128-5 (6-pack)
  1. Forest ecology—Juvenile literature. 2. Forests and forestry—Juvenile literature. 3. Habitat (Ecology)—Juvenile literature. I. Title.
  QH541.5.F6K566 2009
  577.3—dc22
                                            2008023569

Manufactured in the United States of America

CONTENTS

WHAT IS A FOREST HABITAT?

Do not let the word "habitat" scare you. It is just a name for the places where plants and animals make their homes. A desert or a pond is a habitat. A forest is a habitat as well.

All forests are not alike, though. There are many types. Graphic organizers can be a great way to learn about them. You can use a classifying web, for example, to sort facts about different kinds of forests and their plants and animals. In this book, you will find lots of graphic organizers with interesting facts about forest habitats!

The Olympic National Forest, in Washington State, is home to the Roosevelt elk, shown here. This forest is a rain forest, where many plants and animals live.

WHERE ARE THE WORLD'S FORESTS?

Forests are found all around the world. Long ago, they covered about two-thirds of the land on Earth. Today, forests cover about one-third of the land. They are still home to over half of all the kinds of plants and animals on Earth, though!

Some forests are in hot places, and some are in cold places. Some receive a lot of rain, and some get only a little. Some forests receive lots of snow. Some are in places that often have fires. Different kinds of plants and animals live in each sort of forest.

This map shows the main forests in the world in green. There are forests in other places, too, but this map shows the largest areas covered in forest.

Map: Forests Around the World

Major forested areas on Earth

FALLING LEAVES

You may have seen trees with leaves that turn bright colors in the fall. These are **deciduous** trees. Their broad leaves turn red, orange, yellow, or brown every fall, then drop off. New leaves grow in the spring.

Forests that have mostly trees like this are called deciduous forests. They are found in places that have four seasons, with warm summers and cold winters.

Deciduous forests have five **layers**. At the top are the tallest trees. Below them are shorter trees. Next come bushes. Then there are grasses and wildflowers. The bottom layer is moss and **lichen**.

This cycle organizer shows the seasonal cycle of a deciduous tree. This cycle repeats every year in deciduous forests.

Cycle Organizer: A Deciduous Tree Through the Year

SPRING

Leaves begin to appear

SUMMER

Leaves have fully grown in

WINTER

Leaves are gone

FALL

Leaves change color and begin to fall off the tree

NEEDLE LEAVES

Be careful if you touch the leaves of a **conifer**! Its thin, pointed leaves are as sharp as needles and may stick your finger. The word "conifer" means "cone-bearing." These trees have cones that hold their seeds. Since the trees are green all year, they are also called evergreens.

Forests with mostly conifers are called coniferous forests. They are found in places that have long winters with lots of rain or snow. Coniferous forests have fewer layers than deciduous forests. There is only one tree layer, with a few bushes or small plants below it. Mosses and lichens cover the ground.

This Venn diagram shows how deciduous and coniferous forests are alike and different. The things that are alike are listed where the two circles overlap.

Venn Diagram: Comparing Deciduous Forests and Coniferous Forests

DECIDUOUS FOREST

- trees have broad leaves
- leaves turn colors in fall
- leaves drop off in fall
- found in places with four clear seasons
- rich soil
- tall trees and short trees
- grasses and wildflowers
- lots of sunlight reaches ground

BOTH

- found in Europe, Asia, and North America
- trees are main plants
- layers
- bushes, mosses, and lichens

CONIFEROUS FOREST

- trees have needles
- needles stay green
- always needles on trees
- found in places with long winters with lots of rain or snow
- poor soil
- all trees are equally tall
- little sunlight reaches ground

A SPECIAL FOREST: THE RAIN FOREST

As you can tell from its name, a rain forest gets a lot of rain. There are **tropical** rain forests near the **equator**. There are also **temperate** ones in cooler places. Some rain forests get about 5 feet (1.5 m) of rain each year. In others, the yearly rainfall may be more than 33 feet (10 m)!

Very tall trees, up to 200 feet (61 m) tall, grow in rain forests. Little sunlight reaches the ground. The few plants that grow on the forest floor must have large, flat leaves to catch as much sunlight as they can.

This bar graph shows the amount of rain that fell each month in Mount Waialeale rain forest in 2006. This forest is one of the rainiest spots on Earth!

Bar Graph: Rainfall in Hawaii's Mount Waialeale Rain Forest

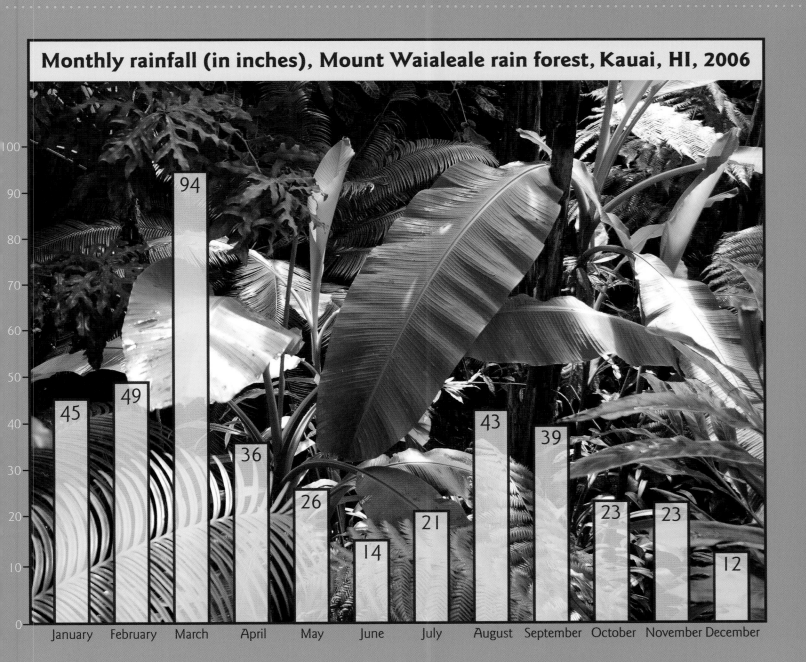

Monthly rainfall (in inches), Mount Waialeale rain forest, Kauai, HI, 2006

Month	Rainfall (inches)
January	45
February	49
March	94
April	36
May	26
June	14
July	21
August	43
September	39
October	23
November	23
December	12

SO MANY TREES!

Did you know that there are about 20,000 kinds of trees? That is a lot of trees! Some are deciduous, such as maple, oak, elm, and willow trees. Others are conifers, such as pine, fir, cedar, and redwood trees. How can you tell which is which? Their leaves can help you tell them apart. You can also look to see if they have cones.

Tropical rain forests have more kinds of trees than any other kind of forest. Rubber, lemons, and oranges all come from trees that grow in tropical rain forests. How many other kinds of trees can you name?

This star diagram gives facts about redwood trees. Redwood forests grow naturally along the coast from Oregon to California.

Star Diagram: Redwood Trees

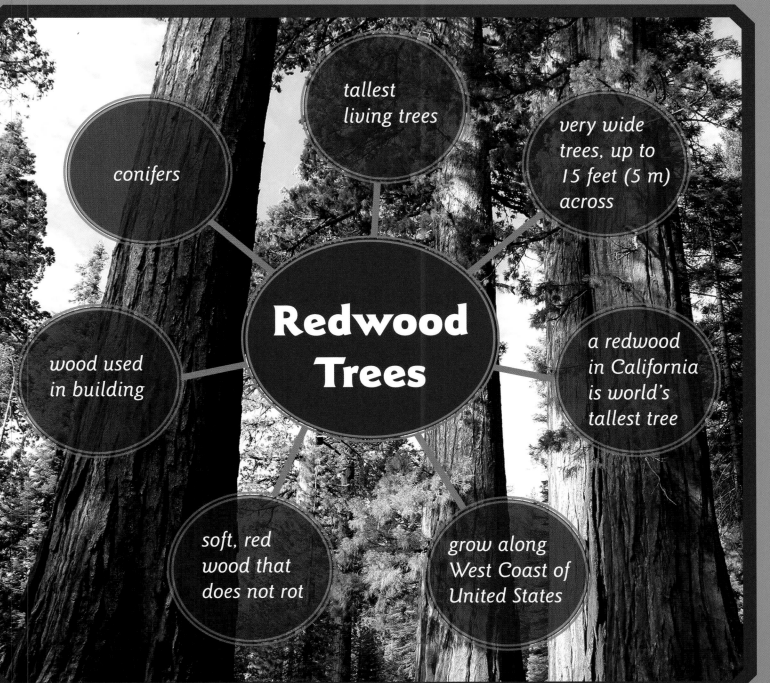

Redwood Trees

- tallest living trees
- very wide trees, up to 15 feet (5 m) across
- conifers
- wood used in building
- a redwood in California is world's tallest tree
- soft, red wood that does not rot
- grow along West Coast of United States

MORE THAN JUST TREES

There is more to a forest than just trees. Deciduous forests have many kinds of plants because lots of sunlight reaches the ground. There are bushes, grasses, and wildflowers. Mosses and lichens grow, too.

Coniferous forests and rain forests have fewer plants because little sunlight reaches the ground. Rain forests, however, often have vines that reach sunlight by climbing up the trees. They also have special plants called **epiphytes** that grow high in the trees. Epiphytes' roots do not need soil. They get their food from the air!

Concept webs show how many ideas or topics can be connected. This concept web shows all the different kinds of plants that can grow in a forest.

Concept Web: Forest Plants

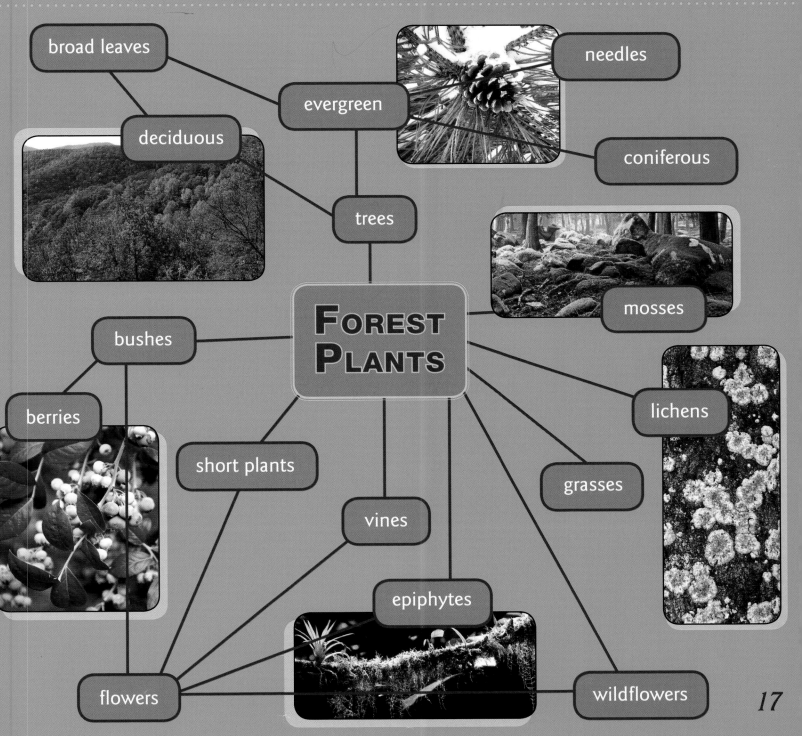

broad leaves

needles

evergreen

deciduous

coniferous

trees

mosses

FOREST PLANTS

bushes

lichens

berries

short plants

grasses

vines

epiphytes

flowers

wildflowers

ANIMALS IN FOREST HABITATS

Take a walk through a forest, and you might see some of the animals that call it home. Forests supply food and places to live for all sorts of animals.

Watch the ground. You may see small animals such as bugs, frogs, snakes, lizards, chipmunks, or squirrels. There may be foxes, raccoons, or porcupines as well. Look up in the trees, and you may see birds or bats. Tropical forests have monkeys in the trees, too!

Lots of larger animals also live in forests. You might find deer, bears, or wolves. Some forests in Africa and Asia even have elephants or tigers!

This cluster map shows facts about many large animals that live in forests. For example, the moose lives in coniferous forests, has fur, and eats plants.

Cluster Map: Large Forest Animals

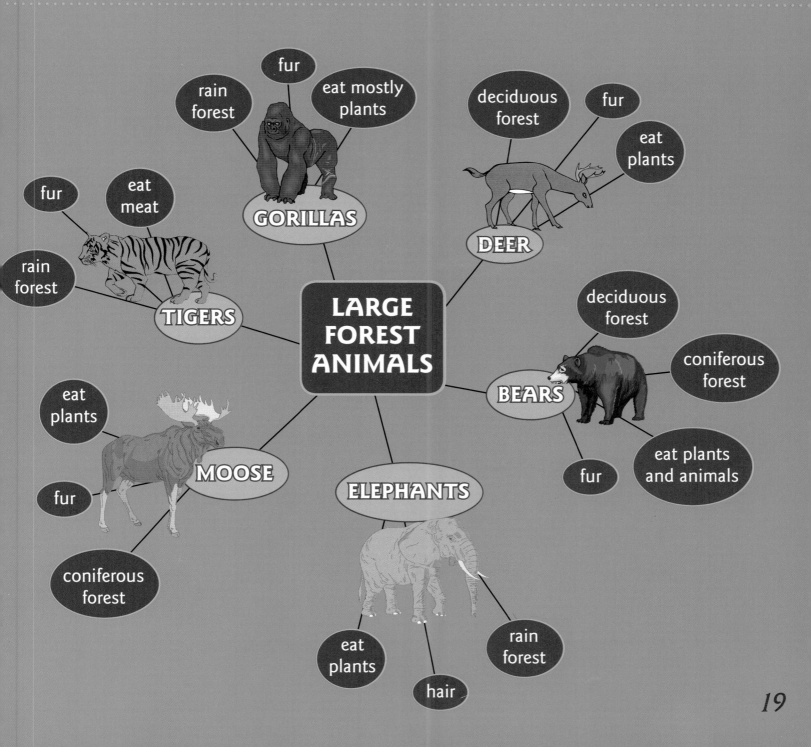

fur

rain forest

eat mostly plants

GORILLAS

deciduous forest

fur

eat plants

DEER

fur

eat meat

rain forest

TIGERS

LARGE FOREST ANIMALS

deciduous forest

coniferous forest

BEARS

fur

eat plants and animals

eat plants

fur

coniferous forest

MOOSE

ELEPHANTS

eat plants

hair

rain forest

A CLOSER LOOK: THE RACCOON

Have you ever seen an animal wearing a black mask? If it had a ringed tail, it was likely a raccoon. Raccoons live in forests, among other places.

Raccoons often make their dens in trees. They sleep during the day and move around at night. They eat almost anything, including plants, bugs, and small animals.

Babies are born in the spring. After a few months, they begin going out at night with their mothers. She teaches them how to feed themselves and stay safe. They remain with her for many months. Raccoons are an important part of the forest habitat!

This fishbone map shows facts about a raccoon's body, such as its size and markings. Using the map, can you find out how many toes a raccoon has?

Fishbone Map: A Raccoon's Body

FUR
- Long
- May be different colors
- Gray or brown
- Mask on face is black

PAWS
- Five toes with sharp claws on each paw
- Back paws longer than front paws
- Use front paws like hands
- Pick up food to put it in mouth

A RACCOON'S BODY

SIZE
- 24 to 42 inches (61–107 cm) long, with tail
- Weigh from 7 to 40 pounds (3–18 kg)
- Males larger than females

TAIL
- Bushy
- May be as long as body
- Five to seven rings
- Rings are black

PEOPLE AND FORESTS

Forests are not just for plants and animals. People need forests, too! The trees and plants in forests produce much of the **oxygen** that people need to breathe. Rain forests have given us many drugs for treating illnesses. However, people are putting forests in danger. In some places, people are cutting down too many trees. People also cause **pollution**, which hurts forests and the plants and animals that live there.

Forests are important. We need to keep them healthy. Can you think of ways for people to take care of forests? Use what you know about graphic organizers to make one that shows people how they can help Earth's forests!

GLOSSARY

conifer (KAH-nih-fur) A type of tree that has needlelike leaves and grows cones.

deciduous (deh-SIH-joo-us) Having leaves that fall off every year.

epiphytes (EH-puh-fyts) Plants that grow on other plants and get what they need to make food from the air and rain.

equator (ih-KWAY-tur) The imaginary line around Earth that separates it into two parts, northern and southern.

layers (LAY-erz) Levels of something.

lichen (LY-ken) A plant that is made of algae and fungi. Algae are plantlike living things without roots or stems that live in water. Fungi are plantlike living things that do not have leaves, flowers, or green color and that do not make their own food.

oxygen (OK-sih-jen) Gas that has no color or taste and is necessary for people and animals to breathe.

pollution (puh-LOO-shun) Man-made waste in air, soil, and water that hurts living things.

temperate (TEM-puh-rut) Not too hot or too cold.

tropical (TRAH-puh-kul) Having to do with the warm parts of Earth that are near the equator.

INDEX

WEB SITES

Due to the changing nature of Internet links, PowerKids Press has developed an online list of Web sites related to the subject of this book. This site is updated regularly. Please use this link to access the list:
www.powerkidslinks.com/graphoh/forest/